bad astrocyte

ALSO BY CAMERON MORSE

Far Other by Woodley Press

Baldy by Spartan Press

Coming Home with Cancer by Blue Lyra Press

Terminal Destination by Spartan Press

Father Me Again by Spartan Press

Fall Risk by Glass Lyre Press

Bad Astrocyte

poems

Cameron Morse

Woodley Press

2021

Printed in the United States of America

Published by Woodley Press, Washburn University, Topeka, KS

Cover art: Cameron Morse, Kathleen Greeson, Ashlea Hodges

Typesetting, layout, and cover design: Cameron Morse, Greg Field

ISBN: 978-1-7360366-0-0

Library of Congress Cataloging-in-Publication data

Woodleypress.org

for the diagnosed

ACKNOWLEDGMENTS

A hearty thanks must go to the members of the Facebook group, "GBM SURVIVORS TO THRIVERS," from whose personal accounts many of these poems derive inspiration; to intrepid photographer Kathleen Greeson and her subject Ashlea Hodges for the use of the photograph on the cover; Al Ortolani and the folks at Woodley Press for believing in this book, editing and seeing it through the various stages of production; Kari Ann Ebert and Stephen Scott Whitaker for featuring a few bits of the project on The Broadkill Review podcast and for being willing to enter this venture with me along with the editors of the following magazines in which these poems first appeared (some in earlier forms):

Brickplight : "Toxicity," "Declining," "Functionality"
The Broadkill Review: "Stiletto," "Vector," "Magnetic Moments"
Constellations: "Night Fright"
Eunoia Review: "Sno-Storm," "75%"
Fomer People: "Harmonic Tune," "Apoptosis"
indicia: "Handling Pills," "Parent Child Interaction Therapy"
The Metaworker: "The Surgeon"
The Opiate: "Night Feed"
The Pangolin Review: "My Octopus Teacher"
Poetry Super Highway: "Temporal"
Quail Bell: "Inspirational Space"
Rogue Agent: "Piece of Mind"
Sprung Formal: "Growing Theo," "Just Breathe"
Sweet Tree Review: "HALOS"
Thimble: "Glioblastoma Facts"
Verdad Magazine: "Side Effects"

Glioblastoma is a highly malignant brain tumor that arises from astrocytes, the supportive cells in the nervous system

CONTENTS

I

II

TEMPORAL

In the temple the dark
chapel of cloudy
morning but also that other
world incessantly
set up against one that is
only temporary

I have a bone
to pick with you

          *

Theo literally holding
himself his pee

a very busy young man
my neurosurgeon:

right temporal
lobe grade
IV

glioblastoma

          *

Children sprout

from my seed
seedlings

stem cells

responsible for

a high rate
of recurrence

*

Thought you were a penne guy
now you're going
full-blown rotini on me

*

Translating the hand
me down chains
of carbon from sausage

links into neuronal
currents the currencies
of language of

lightbulb!

2

MY OCTOPUS TEACHER

Imprint me
Mother with your figure

Slats of light
from the slammed Venetian blind

      *

Side effects of decreased appetite
generalized weakness

Curling fetal
on the kitchen floor

on Keppra
among the tight cabinets

      *

Gifts unwrapped
an aftermath of wrapping paper

Day after Christmas
we dismantle the artificial tree

peel the label that says
"Virginia pine"

      *

3

Side effects of irritability
indifferent behavior
agitation

a lull in the traffic
of neurotransmitters

I grip Theo's wrist
hurry across
a hush of fallen leaves

                 *

Pressed into pressure
weighed into
weight

an octopus cradling
its leg stump

4

GLIOBLASTOMA FACTS

Median survival after diagnosis 15 months

    *

So finally accountable
for the clogged
toilet

even when the rubber
block or Matchbox
car obstructing water
flow wasn't yours

and the seizure came
out of nowhere

    *

5 year survival rate just 5 percent

    *

Throwing Grandpa
Bonnard's shaving brush
down the laundry

chute   pinging
off the basket below

sailing a cousin
across the condominium
on a TV tray

cherished childhood memories
pandemonium

*

Current standard of care consisting of surgery
radiation and chemotherapy
is not effective

*

The Home Depot
stroller streaking
behind Theo's
dinosaur rain jacket

cradling the crisp
new blinds in long boxes
stark contrast
to the snaggled slats

at home admitting
light mouthfuls   of broken light

APOPTOSIS

Theo detrains
from the polyester
plush throw

proceeds to skip his nap

           *

Programmed cell death
forced leave retirement
the tired cells   shut down

power cells one by one
blinking out all over
the horizon   event horizon

           *

           *Don't stay awake
           for too long don't go to bed
           I'll make a cup of*

           *coffee for your head
           I'll get you up and going
           out of bed*

           *

I don't obey my death order
I hibernate
                in the bear cave

7

in the cavern await
our rendezvous a secret
pact between us

I senesce   secreting always toxic
compounds
          crunching the cancer stems
in my mouth
          a landfill for
necrotic roses

          *

Extricating myself now
          more easily

since renaming naptime
          "quiet time"

Theo will sleep

Fizzling out at night
whatever climax
was nigh slips away
an electric eel

Wiggling the prongs
      in an outlet
the bygone power cord
      charge down

            *

Life insurance
willing to pay out
75% for living
people with GBM

With the money
they go to Disney
Mecca for three
fourths already dead

            *

In the morning Lili
complains I got
      the seam wet

      the gap between
sink and countertop

washing strawberries
    for breakfast

              *

A tornado siren
roaring out of nowhere

rips open the sky's blue
envelope

              No symptoms

then
the tumor ten
years undiscovered
finally revealed

              O the melodrama
the phantom unmasked

SOUND BITES

A cancer that begins
in the brain
becomes synonymous
with the brain

an ingrown toenail
total eclipse

      *

Hurrying to clear the concrete
pad before the next
snowfall Lili folds herself
into the crawlspace

with a tiny toy shovel

      *

Snow falls in Weather

my iPhone in direct contradiction
to the stock-still standing sky

digital flakes
bytes   a unit of memory

      *

11

I call my phone
on your phone

I call myself
from every room
in the house
hearing nothing

I do not answer

*

Things turn up in the loam

each object with its own
karmic weight

a dog chain baby
spoon green cigarette
lighter still flicks

flame of the previous
occupant fallen
through the deck boards

HANDLING PILLS

Who ever heard of
cancer catching

a secondhand cancer

caught from linens
the toilet seat lid

    *

Snowplows swoop
down Lynn up
Liberty skipping
our street completely

disconnected as it is
from the main arteries

    *

Use a rubber during
"sexy time"

Touch sparingly
the spit up
basin

    *

Roughening nights
a cascade of wet
beddings

an array of laundry baskets

I curse myself
for checking the diaper
with my finger

checking the furnace
with my finger

*

Bathroom mirror

as if choice
steers us
clear

of time and opportunity
I marry myself

each morning by
no choice of
my own

GADOLINIUM

A liver cell may stray
replicate a liver
in the lung

Am I alive
in this confection
called cancer

I am a liver

    *

Gadolinium may stay

several months
or years in the body

an unwanted house
guest gadfly

    *

Is a silvery white metal
when oxidation is
removed

frosted shingles downhill
along 41st Terrace

Smoke following
the wind falls

from the chimney cap

  *

The killer flays skin into angel wings
and suspends them using
fishing wire

His victims guard him
while he sleeps

  *

Socrates imbibed the hemlock
  prescribed him

I premedicate for another scan

  High contrast

  *

Yellow vomit on the motel
room alarm clock

reveals the killer has the same
brain tumor I do

TOXICITY

Because side effects
of the contrast
agent used in MRI's

are also symptoms of
the tumor the MRI's are
designed to track

I am either/or
all the time   I lie
awake reviewing

my life's most
cringeworthy episodes

its cliffhanger ending

       *

Gadolinium hangover
drug stored in my
blood since yesterday
junk yard slung

My new medical—not
neuro—oncologist's
name I hear pronounced
in the virtual waiting
room: "Mehta"

as in narrative

17

"virtual" as in reality

       *

Leafy vortex
      of the driveway

shriveled whirlwind

   Grit
of coffee grounds
or actual dirt in my mouth

how to tell the difference

IMAGO

Always thinner on film
than I imagine

a spindly spider man
Daddy longlegs

       *

A nurse collecting

testimonies about body
image in the neuro
oncology field

pins down the details
in the glass box
of my iPhone

her butterfly collection

       *

Chrysalis
cracked open

some final version
a director's cut

exclusive interview

*

Imago   I
phone apple ID

face
Book profile

self-identity theft
family tree

*

On steroids
avoid mirrors

a void where once
I saw myself

defined flexed
active gym

member now moon
face pregnant

SNO-STORM

Angling feet into a rattle
of chain between
fenceposts

I sprain my ankle   agèd
without   wisdom

      *

3:36 a.m. Lili shakes my leg

      ice rain at
      the window a
      sheet of cellophane

crinkling   shaken   shiny

    cellulose
an inert carbohydrate
    cellophane a trademark

      *

It's New Year's

I'm too old for the dark
French Roast

make me Comfort Coffee

      *

Collateral Beauty (2016)
I am Will Smith's worst movie
Will Smith's snuffed out
daughter   glial

   celled to death

Why did it get made
asks a top critic

How much did its gifted
cast of big

names have to be paid

      *

Me: *you lie down in clean snow and flap
your arms like this*

     Theo: *you fall down
     there's no angel like that*

NIGHT FEED

The car's scary I'm
scared the car's jumping
over the van taking
me away from mommy
and daddy the car's
turning into the dark

Dear tantrum
dear night terror

we have a hostage situation

    *

Night of disrupted
sleep breach
of insomnia I hold
my shocked
awake inconsolable
infant daughter
to my chest

Overloaded
the mistake I made
with the washing machine

trapped in the same
broken cycle

    *

After eight years on Keppra
I'm tired allll
the time

my patience wares way
too thin

and now the garden hose
won't straighten

kinked in my burning
fingers   freezer
burnt umber red

    Were endless wares
of patience stock

    piled within me I too
could coil a snake

       *

The hive mind or is my mind
a hive of stinging
volts   voltas

a crackling static's *zap!*
ungrounded outlets

       *

Like how many chickens
must be pressure

cooked to mush
how many tons of goop
a day to keep this

human race in business

*

Or *the sun's harmful rays*

just contemplate that phrase

PIECE OF MIND

Wild blueberries smeared
on the faces of

    my kids

invented the yogurt
mustache

       *

Inoperable, methylated wild
    type GBM

reckless bombardier

    Completely shattered

Any bible verses, books, etc.
helped get somewhat of
a piece of mind?

Still am picking up
the pieces   of   my mind

      *

fab lab

18 WOOD WHEEL PCS

For indoor decorative purposes only

If I only knew what
my purpose was
if life was
more than feeling fab
lab rat

      *

Shaking suds
out of my yellow
sponge in the dark wok
water   nonstick

sticking to me
this celebration of
life is also

 death's kazoo a

DEAD END & the railroad
spikes we carry home
from the tracks

      *

*Don't step on the ice walk
on the rocks*

That helps the helpless father
figure prefigured

by my father before me

27

JUST BREATHE

What's real what's
real Omi what's Omi
in the water what's
breaking down the wood

*

White Noise Black
Screen Rain

Thunder Sounds Rain

on Window
with Thunder Mother
Baby Soft White

Mozart Studying Noise
Alpha Waves Stress
Relief Remove

Mental Blockages
Subconscious
Negativity

*

What's caught
in the toilet

what block
in the sinuses

by flashlight
revealed

a small box of
Vaseline

*

Bailing the bowl
down to dregs
of brown water
with a measuring cup

a true friend

*

Unlocking energy
hidden chains
of carbon

don't think am I
hungry any
more

I am high
speed chemicals
expanding

29

gases given off
as heat given
off as light

PARENT CHILD INTERACTION THERAPY

Cars babble
in the cartoon

their language
interpreted
by a judgy

narrator god
a nasally
voice
          [over]
with all the answers

                    *

All fours teeth
clenched
Theo charges
Omi taking
her first shaky
steps arms
outstretched
for balance open
for embrace

                    *

Does he mistake
my calm for
indifference even
permission

I tell myself
to breathe he's
only mining
for attention

negative attention
nonetheless

*

*Thank you for being
a good listener*

the giraffe tells
my son therapist

Britney's hand
shoved up its bum

on the iPhone
before she goes

dark wanting
to watch unnoticed

to examine
our interactions

*

Britney whispering
through me
the wire

I'm wearing

32

I'm not supposed
to be aware I'm wearing

POP SONG

Lili belting
hey Jude
from the bathroom

Theo from his
booster seat
copy-cats:

*take a poop song
and make it
better*

                *

Hard to imagine
a better place

but we are always
going to one

in the mouths of
the people

we leave behind

                *

You can stop
matching your socks now

You can stop folding
your underwear

*

Pick a still point

fencepost chimney
stack doghouse

Don't skip ahead
or lag behind

You may
have to stand still
a long time
before you reach the end
of the train cars
passing

octogenarian

35

SIDE EFFECTS

Antarctic shotgun
tundra blasting
white sand

      fiber in my eyes
      [fiber optics]

layers of snow
flayed from roofs

      Shelter in the shed
      with Theo

overwhelmed

      *

Symptom or side effect
I am   beside
myself I am not my
self right now

washing machine
repeating the same cycle
endlessly

spinning draining rinsing
again   again   &

how much riced
cauliflower will I scrape

with my bare hands
out of the sink

I poured it into before
I sink my head

into the polyester flap
of my bathrobe

before I bury my face
in its fuzzy wing

*

The self I am not I am

       beside
       I am bed   side

or at some unknown
proximity

A Ghost Story

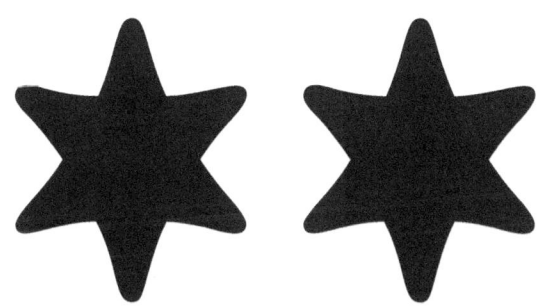

KANSAS CITY ZOO

Terra Cotta Warrior Replicas
donated

one of the largest lion prides
in N. American Zoos

*

How many brushes
with death

does it take
to complete a portrait

of rosebushes

*

Jimmy the Chimp
dies in cage
age 41

Lorikeet exhibit dedicated
to loneliness

Polar Bear Passage
breaks ground

*

41

Mashed scrota
mandarin orange slices

my year-old
presses from mouth
to the pouch

of her rubber bib

       *

Berlin the polar
bear born the year

the wall came down
paces plate glass

greenhouse gases
on her plaque

symbolized by
arrows

the zigzag
zap of a ray gun

       *

Snowmelt morning
another MRI

my three-year-old
lets me in

the back deck sliding glass
iced boards a stack
of cards

a deck stacked against me
my survivability

STILETTO

from *stylus*

writing utensil
once applied to wax
tablet incises

Its blunt end rubs out
an endless erasure

*

Gary Snyder:

the human psyche remains at best
a kind of   Paleolithic thing

*

Electric fish jam each other's
signals   mating calls
sing electric
songs

When Dylan goes electric

the guitar vibrates
a frequency
of sex

44

*

The forensic scientist can't quite make out
the letter tops of *TATTLER*

Will Graham's home address

*

The foot soles of elephants
say hello in another
sensory domain

*

Other vocabs from Brett
Ratner's *Red
Dragon*

sundowner   chinwag   gumshoe

SUPPLEMENTS

Focal   seizure
the point
he swivels around

the small smell
whiffs of
whatever trail he's

picking up on
whatever narrative
thread lost   trailhead

       *

A warrior forages
wild mushrooms

Peels   slices   lets sit
cloves of garlic

The wild patient
enumerates wilderness

    turkey tail lion
    mane milk
    thistle blackseed

Combs the understory
with the burred net
of his beard

       *

Snowstorm day of
the big feast
I tend to

    the oven's tray
of browning potatoes

while Lili showers
then dries her
hair

    wrapped in a towel

      *

One tumor shrinks
half the size
of a pea
a princess wouldn't feel
      aching
in her right hemisphere

Another balloons
a pumpkin in
a patch of pumpkins

    It's time to eat

THE SURGEON

If I check my Facebook
for likes I must want
to be liked   but why

no one who sends me
wishes knows my birthday

       *

   Would you operate
   a second time if
   the surgeon says there
   is no point

       *

What have I created
Lili jokes

Theo cowled in
nylon pterodactyls

head bowed upon
the iPhone   in his hand
climbs into the car seat

zombified acquiescence

       *

   He says the remaining
   cells will grow back

48

fast and why lose time in bed
recovering

the same old territory

   *

Most of my junk
mail penile

dysfunction editors
rejecting my
poetry

  Who will disciple me
  now that my youth

  pastor has moved
  to Arkansas

VECTOR

Theo and I cross
the tracks

"Theodore" Greek
for gift   birth

day present from a god
I don't believe in

three-year-old
theodicy

        *

a quantity possessing both
direction and magnitude

represented by an arrow

by a sere vine in sunlight
    climbing

        *

Dog collars tinkle
in the blinding
light   paw

prints in the sidewalk
wet cement down
to the toenails

clickety-clack   movable type

*

Woodsy interstice
train tracks

Theo forages a rail
road spike

a strikethrough
~~transgression~~

*

Every time we pass
the same white cotton yellow
grass bird's nest

Theo collects another
of the shattered
green pieces of a toy
assault rifle

as if gluing it
back at home   resurrecting
the original impulse

GROWING THEO

Some terrifying
cartoon villain

> what animal was it
> thin strand of
> memory

Carface leering
on Pinterest

*

Lili broke up
with her first boyfriend
because he was short

She hopes to grow Theo
taller than me
as a precaution against
breakups

as if genes had
nothing much to say

*

Forfeited treatments
hospice   age 27

Camo lining his casket
implies a return
to nature

open season

"forfeited" a game
a big game
animal

    perhaps even a crime

     *

Age 27 I too am
surprised
I am

not the animal I expected

MEMORY LOSS

Jumbled conversations
a kind of Jenga
of the mind

each word   perched

plank gingerly laid
          upon plank

*

Debulked but due
to size could not complete

the sentence
resection of the section

you remember best
a partial print

on the eyeball of the victim

*

Lili asks if my left

grip's loosening
my hold

on the world
I inhabit

our world
trying to get pregnant

> *

Blank of memory loss
lost dog of the self

that library book
you returned or so
you swear on the phone
with the librarian

asking her to check the shelf

GRAVITY

Weight as yearning
as the waiting
room

  Heavyhearted

the long wait
for word

     of any kind

      *

Tidal drag
of his blankie

trailing behind
emblematic

of his attachment
to the Earth

Icarus with his
blue whales

print providing
the moniker

     "whales"

*

Teleologically
I am drawn
to you

the draw   drawn
shawl of moonlight
a drippy faucet

of thoughts
I can't turn off

*

Gravity bows
the bookshelves

with books on parenting

*Breakthrough the Whole
Brained Aroma
Therapy Emotionally
Intelligent Diapers
to Dating How to Talk
so Kids Will Listen*

*

Theo wakes up
crying incoherently

57

Idiot standing
at the door

I listen for a reason

INSPIRATIONAL SPACE

Smidgen of snow
in the shadow
of my north-facing house

a holdout from weeks ago
weirdly individual
indivisible

      *

Lot of death posts
in this "positive

hopeful & often
inspirational
space"

enough bedposts
to make a bed
out of death

& lie down in it
but I won't lie down

I will stand up in my death

      *

    Your lunch is [pre

determined by
breakfast] leftover
quiche

*

Father quiet doesn't say much

Needs—or do I?—
need activities to keep him
busy   his mind
occupied

See him sitting
staring into blank space

uninspired   spirited

away
        away

DECLINING

Father on the decline
declines any
further treatments

Goes down
hill with his back turned

verbs away from verbs
their tedium of

unnecessary verbiage
declensions

     *

My hands shake
   randomly

When I try to type

my fingers fall
all over the keyboard

   the pattering
typography of   rain

     *

In the olden days
Mavis Beacon

Teaches [or   taught?]
Typing

Dad prissily
postured

fingers arched

above the buttons
correctly

assigned to a
s d f

        j k l ; an attorney
who had required a typist

            *

Father
Christmas God the
Father all
those upper case
letters

        May
you end by locking up
yourself in self
doubt   in ALL CAPS

        May I

HALOS

GBM SURVIVORS TO THRIVERS

I said goodbye to

my sister   this morning

collected her angel wings

*

California mandarins

sweet • seedless • easy peel

*

This morning tore

open her ocean   spray

*

Amtrack a quick
rustle in interstitial trees

three four cars
frosted passenger windows

passing past passed away

*

My father from the sunshine

state my infant father
daughter gumming

the translucent sac
tonguing pulpy globs

toward the crumb catcher

       *

This morning
the promised snow

fall fell felled

My sister slept
on a cloud

       *

Omi greens the sleeve
of my hoodie

avocado finger grit
catches me

mopping her tray

FUNCTIONALITY

Scrutinizing me
at breakfast

Lili stares while I
drag avocado

peel over the hook
of my left hand

scraping sliced
green meat

over the curled
fingers she insists

I'm losing the use of
out of laziness

       *

March charm

      wearing off?
This tiny
spot   signifying
a turn   in the poem

another bird
house dropped
during last night's
thunderstorm

*

Omi's glass jar tosses
milk splatter

Both hands!

She lays it down
at the table's edge

*

Woodpecker
confirmed

origin of the inside
of a barrel
drum

startled drilling for
gutter ants

angles again
for the gutter

the moment
I close the door

an eternal recurrence

HARMONIC TUNE

For my 34th birth
day we hang harmonically
tuned tubes from
a rafter in the eaves   wind
chimes our infernal
woodpecker's undeterred by
headbanging our north
gutter corner
a coroner reporting gunshots
at all hours of the day
gunshot reports

     *

From the Tibetan
Book of Living
       and Dying

Ethan Sisser's "death
doula" with
the pierced nostril
reports him surrounded
at home   hospice
by chanting   incense

   day 12 without food
without water bedridden
faint of breath
quiet pulse   "dropping
his body"

67

his botched skull
black goatee

*

When Theo decides
to go back to the Montessori
on my birthday
to terrorize his teachers
for a change
I recover my breath
for the first time in weeks
Omi's white noise
machine a waterfall cascading

in the stillness
of shattered lampshades
all those snapped
harps   harps[ichords]

NIGHT FRIGHT

I want to preserve
mental toughness persevere
for the sake of my children
choose caution without fear
as if that were a thing   it is
though isn't it like walking
on the sidewalk   locking up
the doors before bed just
in case the things you aren't
afraid of won't happen
because you took precautions

*

I wanted to believe the rainbow
overarching 41st Street was
opening the back door of our Toyota
Sienna in lieu of an umbrella
with Omi in my arms I wanted to
believe in sign language
because the sparks of rain falling
in the setting sun were
the setting sun because the clouds
(and believe me I know how
cliché this all is, you heartfelt vampires
seeking your bills of always
authenticity) the clouds had opened
like a wound and the sun had come out
(there it is   I said it) you see
not even I will get away with this

*

Remembering numerous fingers
especially Salacz's fingers
crossing my line of sight he said
to smile to stick out my tongue
at him and squeeze his fingers
testing my grip I get scared
because of COVID-19 but not
in the way you'd expect I
haven't squeezed in a while

Lie awake gripping my own wrist
right hand then left   testing

*

I don't think I'll ever sleep again

        I'll write my way
through this or at least all the way
up to the edge

                and jump

TUMOR PROGRESSION

Progress I joke
when the hospitalist

on duty arrives
with the results of my
emergency scan

*Dr. Salacz always
so pleased with my progress*

*won't like this now
that I am progressing*

*

On the brown couch
below the magnolia
blooming across 41st

St. Theo lowers his
head in ardent study
of the iPhone in his lap

my iPhone a cartoon
parable of talking trucks

*I hear lightning I hear
a living engine*

*

Approximations of
sprinkler fire
falling over the sidewalk
Donna's gravel drive

I charge the spigot
sidestepping rainbow
spray to tweak
the circumference of waterfall

my treatment plan for
the new seed a news feed
that leaves me starving
because I'm too afraid to eat

MAGNETIC MOMENTS

The Survivor Tree holds the sheet
on Enforceable Statements
to the refrigerator door

*I'll be glad to discuss this
with you as soon as
the arguing stops*

      *

Leaky pineapple blood
vessels and hell

I'd settle for a cup
of salami and cheese

cubes from the hospital cafeteria

      *

*New growth not
encased runs*

*too deep for full
removal, 16 yo son*

*my baby but forceful
adult enough*

to make some decisions

*

Surviving a deluge
of volcanic debris

the tree transported
back to 9/11

*

Bad enough
to have to watch

rhinoceros beetles
wrestle for mating rights

from a movie studio
in the Cotswolds

*

The inverted tree
stands upside-down in a field
of magnets

This occurs to me too
late to make a
difference

Cameron Morse is Senior Reviews editor at *Harbor Review* and the author of seven collections of poetry. His first, *Fall Risk*, won Glass Lyre Press's 2018 Best Book Award. He was diagnosed with an inoperable glioblastoma in 2014, graduated in 2018 with MFA from the University of Kansas City-Missouri and lives in Independence, Missouri, with his wife Lili and two children.

www.ingramcontent.com/pod-product-compliance
Lightning Source LLC
Chambersburg PA
CBHW020731250626
47155CB00006B/2242